ECDL® 5.0

European Computer Driving Licence

Module 7 - Web Browsing & Communication

7a Web Browsing using IE9

Release ECDL279v1

Published by:

      CiA Training Ltd
      Business & Innovation Centre
      Sunderland Enterprise Park
      Sunderland
      SR5 2TA
      United Kingdom

      Tel: +44 (0) 191 549 5002
      Fax: +44 (0) 191 549 9005

      E-mail: info@ciatraining.co.uk
      Web: www.ciatraining.co.uk

      ISBN: 978-1-86005-949-0

First published 2011

Aims

To demonstrate the ability to use web browser application on a personal computer. To understand and accomplish basic operations associated with searching and navigating web sites to access information.

Objectives

After completing the guide the user will be able to:

- Understand what the Internet is and common terms associated with it; be aware of some security considerations when using the Internet. Accomplish everyday web browsing tasks including changing browser settings.

- Complete and submit web-based forms and search for information; save web pages and download files from the web. Copy web content into a document.

Assessment of Knowledge

At the end of this guide is a section called the **Record of Achievement Matrix**. Before the guide is started it is recommended that the user complete the matrix to measure the level of current knowledge.

Tick boxes are provided for each feature. **1** is for no knowledge, **2** some knowledge and **3** is for competent.

After working through a section, complete the **Record of Achievement** matrix for that section and only when competent in all areas move on to the next section.

Contents

Section 1
Getting Started

By the end of this Section you should be able to:

Understand the Internet

Be Aware of Security Issues

Use Internet Explorer

Connect and Reconnect to the Internet

Use Online Help

Be Familiar with the Screens and Views

To gain an understanding of the above features, work through the **Driving Lessons** in this **Section**.

For each **Driving Lesson**, read the **Park and Read** instructions, without touching the keyboard, then work through the numbered steps of the **Manoeuvres** on the computer. Complete the **Revision Exercise(s)** at the end of the section to test your knowledge.

Driving Lesson 1 - Internet Theory

▣ Park and Read

The **Internet** is a vast computer network which allows users all over the world to communicate with each other. The **World Wide Web** (**www**) is not the same thing as the Internet; it is the collection of information that can be accessed via the Internet. This information is stored on web sites (made up of web pages), each of which has a unique address. The **Home Page** of a web site usually consists of an introduction to the site and often contains **hyperlinks** to other pages on that site, or to a different site on the World Wide Web.

Once connected to the Internet, it is possible to publish an individual web site. This is a simple process, as there are now software applications available which make it possible to create a publication without the need to know the Internet programming language, **HTML** (Hypertext Mark-up Language).

Internet Explorer is an application that allows the user to access information on the World Wide Web and to communicate with other users easily. By working through this guide, the user will be ready to access the limitless potential of electronic communication.

Communication

There are many ways to communicate electronically. **E-mail** is a way of sending a message to another computer user anywhere in the world. The message will reach its destination almost immediately. Internet users send and receive e-mail messages by using **e-mail addresses** which, like web site addresses, are unique.

In fact, online communication has opened up entire **virtual communities**. People with similar interests and hobbies can share their views on specifically dedicated web sites. These are known as **Internet forums**, where users hold discussions and post messages on specific subjects.

 Another very popular way of communicating without *a PC is via* **Short Message Service** (**SMS**), *or text messaging between mobile phones.*

Social Networking Sites are used to communicate with other people and share information about yourself online. Some of the most popular sites at the moment are *MySpace*, *Facebook* and *Google+*. These sites can combine many aspects of communication and online communities. Photos and videos can be uploaded for friends to look at, as well as users being able to write blogs and send messages to each other (some messages are like e-mails, but others are like instant messaging systems that can be used to communicate with friends also currently online).

continued over

Driving Lesson 1 - Continued

Instant messaging (**IM**),is a system where two or more users type text and it appears on screen in real time. You always know when your contacts are online, and it's a cheap way of keeping in touch. *Windows Live Messenger* and *Google Talk* are both popular instant messaging programs.

Chat rooms are also popular; these are more informal and a way to meet new friends online. Chat rooms also use **instant messaging** (**IM**), in which two or more users type text and it appears on screen in real time. Many web sites now provide the opportunity for you to play online computer games with other connected users too.

Another way of using the PC as a communication tool is via **Voice over Internet Protocol** (**VoIP**). This works simply by using a microphone and headphones to turn your PC into a phone. You don't pay for calls this way, although some providers do charge a small fee. Examples of VoIP providers are *Skype* and *Google Talk*.

Sharing

There are various ways to publish and share content (such as text, photos, video and audio clips) online:

Web log (**Blog**) - this is a web site where entries are posted in chronological order, like an online diary, or commentary on current affairs. Someone starts the blog and readers can leave comments on the site. A typical blog will contain text, pictures and links to other web pages. Some blogs focus on music, art or photography.

Podcast - this is where media files (audio and video) are broadcast over the Internet. This is a convenient method of receiving music files for example, or for listening to radio programs when it suits you rather than when they are transmitted. A special format of data transfer is used to do this: **RSS feeds** (**Really Simple Syndication**). This format is also used as a way of publishing frequently updated content such as news headlines, football scores, etc. This can be sent directly to your computer or to a device such as a mobile phone. Subscribing to such a service allows you to have the latest version of any specified web page sent to you directly as it changes, without having to seek it out and refresh it.

Be cautious

These online communities can be a fantastic way of making new friends, keeping in touch and having fun. However, you must be aware that not every member of these communities may be genuine - we've all heard of **identity theft**, etc. With this in mind, it's important to take precautions:

♦ Create a private profile to keep your personal information to yourself

♦ Be sparing with the amount of personal information you post, because everything you do post is publicly available

♦ Be very wary of strangers – treat them as you would a stranger you meet on the street.

Driving Lesson 2 - Internet Explorer

▣ Park and Read

Internet Explorer

Internet Explorer 9 is a software application that consists of many components that are designed to allow the user to explore the full potential of the Internet.

The main feature of the package is the **web browser**, which enables the user to "surf the net." The browser facilitates searching for web sites, keeps a record of sites visited and allows favourite sites to be added to a folder for easy access.

IE9 is supplied with *Windows* or can be downloaded from the *Microsoft* web site. There are also other browsers available for PCs, e.g. *Firefox*, Chrome, *Safari* and *Opera*, but only *IE9* is described here.

 This guide has been written assuming that IE9 is running under Windows 7 and all screen shots and options reflect this. It is however possible to run IE9 under other versions of Windows, in which case allowances will need to be made.

 The World Wide Web is constantly being developed. In the lifetime of this guide it is likely that the content of many of the specified web sites may change from that shown here.

Driving Lesson 3 - Security on the Internet

▣ Park and Read

Collecting information

Before using the Internet, especially at home, there are some security implications to be considered. When you access a web site, that site can also obtain information about you and can place files on your computer. This is not always as scary as it sounds. Small text files called **cookies** are stored on your computer when you visit a web site. You can choose whether or not to allow this to happen - whether to allow some, all or none of the files to be stored. However, if you refuse all cookies you may be unable to view some web pages. As you are browsing the Internet a collection of **temporary internet files** is also stored on your computer (in an area known as a **cache**). These speed up the display of pages that you have already visited. The main 'damage' these files (and cookies) do is take up space on your hard drive, but if desired they can be deleted.

Many web sites cannot be accessed without a user name and password; these are called **protected sites**. Sometimes you have to pay a fee up front before you can access a web site, done by entering the user name and password allocated to you. You will usually need a user name and password to shop online at supermarkets such as *Sainsburys* or *Tesco*. Indeed, all networked computers should be protected by a user name and password.

Encryption

A web server/site certificate is obtained by the site owner to verify its identity and encrypt transmissions. This is called a **digital certificate**. Sensitive information passing between you and the target web site is **encrypted** (or scrambled) and can only be deciphered at the target site. Banks that provide an online banking service use extremely high levels of encryption for obvious reasons.

Malware

You should also be aware of potential hazards. Any annoying, hostile or intrusive software or code designed to damage a computer without the owner's knowledge is called **malware** (malicious software). Some files downloaded from the Internet contain **viruses** and other threats, which are programs intended to cause harm to your computer. A specific type of threat is a **worm**; this is a self replicating program which sends copies of itself to linked computers. Another threat is a **Trojan (horse)** which appears to do one thing, but in reality does another, e.g. installs another malicious program. Viruses can be transmitted in this way, but neither a worm nor a Trojan is a virus. **Spyware** is software that is installed without your knowledge. It can monitor your behaviour and collect various types of personal information; it can also change your computer's settings.

continued over

Driving Lesson 3 - Continued

Anti-virus software

Viruses are often attached to e-mail messages. It is vital to have anti-virus software installed and equally important to keep it updated on a weekly basis at least. It is also advisable to use a **firewall**. This is a program that protects your computer from any unauthorised access or intrusion from outside, such as someone trying to access the hard drive to obtain passwords, etc. This type of software is built into **Windows**.

There are many forms of anti-virus software to counter these threats and most PCs have it installed when bought. However, it's extremely important to update it at least on a weekly basis. New threats are developing all the time. You must also perform scans for viruses on a regular basis.

Secure shopping

If you decide to do some shopping on the Internet, make sure you pay using a **secure server**. These web pages can be identified by a small padlock symbol ▢ on *IE9's* **Address Bar** and **https** at the beginning of the address. Unfortunately, there is a small risk of credit card fraud when paying for goods online, but it must be stressed that the risk is really no greater than giving your credit card details to someone in a shop or over the telephone. There are great advantages to shopping online: you don't have to go out and jostle your way through crowds or find city centre parking and it is possible to buy almost anything you can think of from all over the world.

Parental control

There is an unbelievable amount of data on the World Wide Web. There are sites representing every aspect of human life. It follows, then, that there may be content which is offensive to even the most broad-minded person. Indeed, there is some content placed on the web for the sole purpose of being offensive.

Whilst the average person may consider the occasional inadvertent view of offensive material an acceptable price to pay for unrestricted access to the web, there are situations where all possible steps should be taken to prevent this, particularly in the case of access by children. At the time of writing there are no restrictions of any kind built into the Internet; anyone can access anything. There have also been cases of harassment, bullying and, even worse, predators prowling the web to find unsupervised children online. There are, however, external methods of imposing control. Parents can help by physically supervising their children's online time; they can also restrict their browsing, supervise game playing and restrict time spent on the Internet.

If physical supervision is not always possible, Internet browsers (and some firewalls) include content filters, which can allow or restrict access based on a rating system or by individual site. Commercial software is available which will restrict access to sites based on content and by individual site. This software often includes the ability to monitor and restrict chat room access, currently an increasing area of concern.

continued over

Driving Lesson 3 - Continued

Manoeuvres

1. Click the **Start** button, select **Control Panel** and open **Internet Options** (you may need to select the **Network and Internet** category first).

2. Select the **Content** tab of the **Internet Properties** dialog box and look at the buttons in the **Content Advisor** area.

*If **Content Advisor** is currently enabled, there will be a **Disable** button rather than an **Enable** button. If **Content Advisor** has never been activated, the **Settings** button will be unavailable.*

3. To activate the **Content Advisor** settings, click **Enable**. If it has been activated, click **Settings** to amend the options. If prompted, enter the **Supervisor** password and click **OK**.

4. Click on each **Category** and set the **slider** to the required level of access.

5. Click the **Approved Sites** tab and enter addresses (URLs) of specific sites that can **Always** be viewed or **Never** be viewed.

6. Click the **General** tab. There is an option to allow users to see any site that does not have a rating. If this is not selected, only sites with the required ratings can be viewed.

7. There is also a button here to allow the **Supervisor password** to be changed (the original password must be known). Setting a password here for the first time will activate the system. The password is case sensitive.

8. Click **Cancel** to ignore any changes, including activation.

*Only click **OK** to accept the settings and activate the system if you are sure that is what you want. Once activated, the **Content Advisor** system can only be enabled, disabled or amended by using the password.*

9. Close the **Internet Properties** dialog box and the **Control Panel** window.

Driving Lesson 4 - Connecting to the Internet

▣ Park and Read

Before connecting to the Internet, the user must either have a **broadband** (always on) connection or a **dial-up** connection (see next Driving Lesson) available.

Your broadband connection can be supplied using a telephone line, cable or satellite. Sometimes there will be a device (router) that must be switched on to make the connection, sometimes it will be permanently available. Connection between your computer and the broadband system can use cables or can be entirely wireless.

On a network, the Internet connection will probably be made via the server and made available automatically at all networked computers.

It is also necessary to subscribe to an **Internet Service Provider (ISP)**. They handle all the information to and from your computer and provide a connection to the rest of the Internet. They will normally also supply you with a unique **e-mail address**.

↷ Manoeuvres

1. Click the **Start** button from the *Windows* **Desktop** and select **Internet Explorer,**

ℹ️ *Internet Explorer may also exist as a shortcut icon on the **Desktop**, , or the **Taskbar**, .*

2. The *Internet Explorer* window will be displayed. If the connection to the Internet is active the window will show a web page.

ℹ️ *If the connection to the Internet is not active for any reason, an appropriate message will be displayed.*

3. The default starting web page shown whenever an Internet connection is first made is known as your **Home Page**. This guide displays the *Microsoft* site, **msn.com**, as the **Home Page**. However, yours may be different. Leave the default starting web page open.

ℹ️ *It is possible to change your **Home Page** at any time. If you want to change your **Home Page**, go to Driving Lesson 27 and perform steps 1-3, substituting **www.msn.com** for the site of your choice.*

Driving Lesson 5 - Dial-up Connection

🅿 Park and Read

If there is no broadband connection available, it is possible to have a dial-up connection to the Internet. This usually involves having a **modem** installed or connected to the computer. This is a device that converts signals from the computer into signals that can travel through a phone line. Using a dial-up connection takes over exclusive use of a telephone line whilst connected, so normal voice calls will not be possible on that line while the Internet is being used.

This Driving Lesson should only be read if using a dial up connection.

Manoeuvres

1. Click the **Start** button from the *Windows* **Desktop** and select **Internet Explorer**, [🌐 Internet Explorer ▸]. If there is not a current connection, the **Dial-up Connection** dialog box will be displayed.

ℹ️ *Depending on the settings on the computer, the connection may be dialled automatically.*

2. The default **Connect to** location will be displayed. The **User name** and **Password** may already be present. If not, when the **Dial-up Connection** dialog box is displayed, enter the relevant **User name** and **Password**. Click on **Connect**.

ℹ️ *Different systems may have different **Dial-up Connection** dialog boxes*

3. The *Internet Explorer* window will be displayed showing your **Home Page** web site as before.

ℹ️ *The connection may be lost for technical reasons or if it has been inactive for a certain length of time. The **Dial-up Connection** dialog box will be displayed again.*

Driving Lesson 6 - Browser Help

▣ Park and Read

Internet Explorer contains an online **Help** facility that may assist when certain problems are experienced.

⌒ Manoeuvres

1. Your default **Home Page** is shown in the *Internet Explorer* window. This will be explained in the next few Driving Lessons.

2. To open the **Help** facility, press the <**F1**> key on your keyboard.

ⓘ *Help can also be accessed from the **Menu bar**, but this is not displayed by default. It will be described later.*

3. The **Windows Help and Support** window is displayed. A **Getting Started** article may be shown on opening, containing links (pale blue or purple) to various other topics. Click any link to display the relevant help, then click the **Home** button, [🏠], to display the **Help** home page.

4. Click the **Browse Help** button, [📖]. This groups the **Help** topics into sections like the chapters in a book and displays the **Contents** page.

5. Click on any section (book) to open it and display a list of topics and further categories. Click on any topic to display help text for that topic in the window, or click any category for a further list of relevant topics (and maybe even more subcategories).

6. Help on specific topics can be quickly located. Type **virus** in the search box at the top and then click the search button, [🔍].

7. A list of topics which contain the search keyword is displayed. Select an entry from the list to display the relevant help text.

8. Click the **Ask** button. A list of additional support options is displayed.

9. Click the **Close** button, [✕], at the top right corner of the **Help** window to close it. Leave the *Internet Explorer* window open.

Driving Lesson 7 - Internet Explorer Screen

🅿 Park and Read

Once the user has made the connection to the Internet, the designated **Home Page** will appear. In this guide we use the **Microsoft** site, **uk.msn.com**, as an example.

🗺 Manoeuvres

1. Look at the screen. This shows the default *IE9* display. At the top of the window are **Navigation** buttons, the **Address bar** (displaying the web address of the site being viewed), the **Tabs** for all open sites, and three tool buttons (**Home**, **Favorites** and **Tools**). The rest of the window displays the current web page.

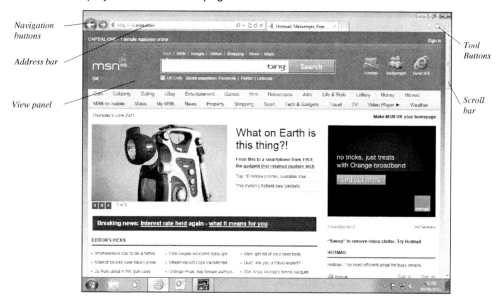

Navigation buttons

Address bar

View panel

Tool Buttons

Scroll bar

ℹ️ *The content in the **View panel** will look different to this, because the content of Microsoft web pages is constantly changing.*

ℹ️ *This is the default view of IE9 but there are many options to vary it which will be described in the next exercise.*

Driving Lesson 8 - Views

 Park and Read

The default view of the *IE9* window has only a single row of controls with the rest of the window showing the selected web page. This maximises the amount of content that can be displayed.

The layout can be varied, however, by adding new components and moving existing features. This will not affect the operation of the application, only how the various features are accessed or displayed. Some of the changes have the effect of reproducing the layout of previous releases of *Internet Explorer*.

One change is to open an area on the left of the screen known as the **Favorites Center**. This allows access to **Favorites** (web pages that are saved and stored by users for quicker future access), **Feeds** (regular updates from frequently updated websites) and **History** (a record of recently visited websites).

Manoeuvres

1.	With your default **Home Page** on the screen, right click on a blank area at the top of the window to display this menu.

2.	Click **Menu bar** to select it. The **Menu bar** is added to the screen. This bar contains menus with commands to control the operation of *IE9* (including a **Help** menu).

3.	Right click again and select **Favorites bar**. This bar can contain buttons which link to your frequently used sites so they can be accessed easily.

4.	Right click again and select **Command bar**. This bar contains buttons with more commands for controlling *IE9*, including some which are also included in the **Menu bar**.

continued over

Driving Lesson 8 - Continued

5.   Right click again and select **Status bar**. This adds the **Status bar** to the bottom of the window, containing current information, including the relevant web address for any link which is selected on the page.

6.   Right click again and select **Show tabs on a separate row**. The tabs for all open sites are now displayed below the **Address bar**. The top of the *IE9* window will now look like this:

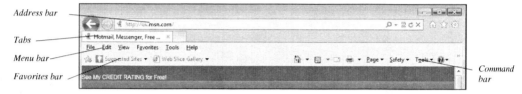

Address bar — *Tabs* — *Menu bar* — *Favorites bar* — *Command bar*

> **i** *Any of these view options can be cancelled by right clicking in the blank area at the top of the window, and clicking an option to deselect it.*

7.   Click **Tools** from the **Command bar** and select **Full Screen** from the menu to remove all bars from the display except the **Status Bar**.

8.   To return to the normal view, move the mouse to the top of the screen until the toolbar reappears, then click the **Restore** button, [icon], in the top right corner of the screen and leave the **Home Page** open.

> **i** *The <F11> key can be used to toggle between **Full Screen** and normal view.*

9.   Click the **Favorites** button, [icon], in the top right of the window, to view the **Favorites Center** in a panel on the right of the main page display.

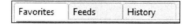

> **i** *The **History** and **Favorites** features will be discussed in greater detail later. Pages listed in the **History** or **Favorites** can be displayed by clicking on them.*

10.   Click anywhere in the main view window to remove the **Favorites Center**.

11.   Click the **Favorites** button again to display the **Favorites Center** and click [icon] to pin it to the left of the window. This means that it will remain on screen until you manually close it. by clicking [X] or you click [icon] again.

12.   Click the **History** tab. The **Favorites Center** panel now displays details of the pages that have been visited recently.

13.   Click the **Favorites** tab.

14.   Close the **Favorites Center** by clicking [X] in the panel or [icon] again.

Driving Lesson 9 - Closing the Browser

▣ Park and Read

To end the current browsing session, the web browser must be closed. With a dial-up connection also make sure the connection is terminated (if you are not prompted to disconnect automatically).

⌇ Manoeuvres

1.   Click the **Close** button, , on the **Title Bar** at the top right corner of the *Explorer* window.

[i]   *Alternatively, select **File** and then **Exit** from the **Menu Bar**, if displayed.*

2.   If you have control over your Internet connection, via a router for instance, you may wish to switch it off at this stage to completely sever the connection. However many applications are designed to operate with an active Internet connection (*Microsoft Office* online help system for example) and it may be advisable to leave the connection in operation.

3.   If you have a dial up connection it is more likely that you will want to close the connection after use. An **Auto Disconnect** dialog box, similar to this, should appear after closing *Explorer*.

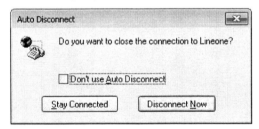

4.   Select **Disconnect Now** to end the current session.

[i]   *If the **Auto Disconnect** dialog box does not appear when using a dial up connection, it is possible to disconnect by clicking the* [icon] *icon on the **Taskbar** and selecting the **Disconnect** option.*

Driving Lesson 10 - Revision

This covers the features introduced in this section. Try not to refer to the preceding Driving Lessons while completing it.

1.   What does **www** stand for?

2.   What is the main programming language used on the Internet?

3.   What must you have before attempting to connect to the Internet?

4.   Use online help to find out about *Microsoft* **Product Updates**.

5.   Which feature can contain details of favourite sites and a history of visited sites?

6.   What additional bars can be included at the top of the *Internet Explorer* window?

7.   Close *Internet Explorer*.

i   *Check the answers at the back of the guide.*

If you experienced any difficulty completing the Revision, refer back to the Driving Lessons in this section. Then redo the Revision.

Driving Lesson 11 - Revision

This covers the features introduced in this section. Try not to refer to the preceding Driving Lessons while completing it.

1.   What do the initials **ISP** stand for?

2.   What is the Internet?

3.   How is the **World Wide Web** different from the Internet?

4.   What are **cookies**?

5.   What does **encrypted** mean?

6.   What is a **firewall**?

7.   How can you determine if a server is secure before attempting to pay for goods online using a credit card?

Check the answers at the back of the guide.

If you experienced any difficulty completing the Revision, refer back to the Driving Lessons in this section. Then redo the Revision.

Once you are confident with the features, complete the Record of Achievement Matrix referring to the section at the end of the guide. Only when competent move on to the next Section.

Section 2 Navigation

By the end of this Section you should be able to:

Use Hyperlinks

Move Backward and Forward through a Web Site

Use Web Addresses

Store and Organise Bookmarks

Use the History Feature

Stop and Refresh Downloads

To gain an understanding of the above features, work through the **Driving Lessons** in this **Section**.

For each **Driving Lesson**, read the **Park and Read** instructions, without touching the keyboard, then work through the numbered steps of the **Manoeuvres** on the computer. Complete the **Revision Exercise(s)** at the end of the section to test your knowledge.

Driving Lesson 12 - Using Hyperlinks

Park and Read

Most web sites contain **hyperlinks**. These are text items, pictures or buttons which, when activated, immediately take the user to a different site, or a different page within the current site.

There is no limit to the number of hyperlinks a web site can have so any site can be linked to many other related sites, each one of which in turn will be linked to many more. This led to the idea of a huge 'web' of information (the World Wide Web). This interconnected mass of information can be browsed relatively simply by choosing a trail of hyperlinks from one site to another.

The advantage of using hyperlinks to navigate within the pages of a single site is that they make it much more interesting and user-friendly.

Manoeuvres

1. Connect to the Internet if necessary, and start *Internet Explorer*.

2. Enter **www.bigplanetsupport.co.uk** in the **Address Bar** and press **<Enter>**. The home page of the site is displayed, <u>replacing</u> the **MSN** site (only one tab is displayed).

3. Click on the link **Hyperlinks** on the left of the screen. A new page is displayed in the main part of the window.

*Notice that the panel with the **Navigation** links remain unchanged when the content in the main window changes. This effect used to be achieved by using **Framed** web pages, but this has been replaced by more modern techniques.*

continued over

Driving Lesson 12 - Continued

4. Read the information that is displayed. If necessary, use vertical scroll bar on the right to view all of the content.

5. Click the word **here** in the third line of the body of the text. This is a hyperlink which opens a new page. Click the link **Return to the previous page** to return to the **Hyperlinks** page.

6. Pictures can be hyperlinks. Click this image on the **Hyperlinks** page to display a new page. Click the link **Return to the previous page** to return to the **Hyperlinks** page.

7. To demonstrate a hyperlink to a new site, click on **Google Search** on the **Hyperlinks** page. The **Google** home page is displayed.

8. *IE9* has **Tabs** to allow different sites to be open at the same time within the same instance of *Explorer*. Notice that there is now a new tab for the **Google** page, but the tab for **bigplanetsupport** is still there.

> The active tab is a different colour and has a *Close* button at the right.

9. The **bigplanetsupport** site is still open; click the **bigplanetsupport** tab to display it.

10. Click the **NASA** link on the **Hyperlinks** page to display the **NASA** home page in another tab. Three tabs are now open.

11. Close the **NASA** tab by clicking its **Close** button (it changes to red, ☒, when the cursor is on it).

> Closing the browser window with more than one tab open displays a message, ***Do you want to close all tabs or the current tab?*** Click ***Close all tabs*** to close the browser and all the tabs, or click the ***Close current tab*** to return to the browser with the other tabs still open.

12. Hyperlinks can be used to open a web page in a new window. Make sure the **Hyperlinks** page of the **bigplanetsupport** site is displayed and right click on the **BBC** link.

13. From the shortcut menu, select **Open in new window**. A new browser window opens containing the new web page.

14. Click the browser **Close** button to remove the window.

15. Click 🏠 to return to your default **Home Page**.

Driving Lesson 13 - Navigation Buttons

P Park and Read

Navigating between web pages/sites in a single tab is made easy by using the

Back, [icon], and **Forward**, [icon], buttons. *Explorer* records the order in which pages are viewed. The **Back** button moves back through the pages until the first page viewed is reached. The **Forward** button moves forward until the most recently viewed page is reached. Holding down either button displays a drop down list of all pages visited before or after the current one. Any page can be selected from the list.

As these buttons only work within a single tab, they are now mostly used to navigate between pages visited in a multi-page site.

Manoeuvres

1. With your default **Home Page** still open, click the **Back** button, [icon]. The screen displays the last page visited.

2. Repeat this action until the button becomes ghosted (pale grey). This means that the first page viewed in this session has been reached and it is impossible to go back any further.

3. Now click the **Forward** button, [icon]. *Explorer* will move forward to the next page in the sequence.

4. Repeat step 3 to move forward through the pages until the **Forward** button is ghosted. This indicates that the most recent page is displayed and it is not possible to go further forward.

5. Click and hold down the **Back** button to reveal a drop down list of all recently visited sites.

6. Click any one to go to it directly.

7. At any time, click [icon] to return to your designated **Home** page.

i *Clicking* [icon] *from the Command bar will also display your designated Home page.*

Driving Lesson 14 - Using Web Addresses

🅿 Park and Read

The quickest and easiest way of visiting a web site is by entering its address, or **URL (Uniform Resource Locator)**, in the **Address Bar**. It is important to ensure that the <u>exact</u> address is entered. Because of the sheer volume of sites on the World Wide Web, it would be almost impossible to locate the required site without a complete address.

A **protocol** is a language that enables computers to speak to one another. **FTP** stands for **File Transfer Protocol**; it is used to make files and folders publicly available for transfer over the Internet. All web sites use the protocol **http (Hypertext Transfer Protocol)**. *IE9* automatically enters the **protocol (http://)**, the type of file to look for. The next part of the address is the **domain name** and is broken up into several segments, separated by periods (full stops). The first is usually **www (World Wide Web)** then a name that often indicates the name of the organisation who owns the site, and then one or more segments indicating the kind of organisation or the country where the server is located, e.g. **com**, **co.uk**, **gov**, etc. Each country has a different last segment of the domain name, e.g. in Australia it is **au** and in Germany it is **de**, so some web addresses will end with these letters.

Every web site has a **Home Page**; this is the first page to appear when the site is opened. This usually consists of a welcome and/or introduction to the site and links to other pages within it. It is different to your default **Home Page**, the page loaded by the **Browser** when it starts or when you press **Home**.

〽 Manoeuvres

1. Click in the **Address Bar** and enter the following address: **www.bigplanetsupport.co.uk** (the address of our support site) then press <**Enter**>. The site is displayed, replacing the previous one.

> ℹ️ *The drop down list on the **Address Bar** can be used to access recently visited sites. Just click on the arrow and select an address from the list.*

2. Browse the details of the site, then click the **Home** button, , to return to your default **Home Page**.

3. In the **Address Bar** type in **www.bbc.co.uk**.

> ℹ️ *Simply entering a search keyword (e.g. BBC) in the **Address Bar** will perform an automatic search and find websites that match.*

4. Hold down the <**Alt**> key and press <**Enter**> to display the site in a new tab.

5. After viewing the details of the **BBC** site, close the tab.

Driving Lesson 15 - Bookmarks

🄿 Park and Read

After using *Internet Explorer* to browse the web, it is likely that the user will have visited some sites that they would like to revisit on a regular basis. *Explorer's* **Favorites** feature provides a quick and hassle free way of doing just that! In a few easy steps favourite sites can be added to a list which, when clicked on, will take the user directly to that site. This is known as **bookmarking** a web page.

Once a list of bookmarks (favourites) has been created, it can be displayed by clicking the **Favorites** button. Any site from the list can then be visited by a click of the mouse.

⌒ Manoeuvres

1.	Click on the drop down arrow of the **Address Bar** and select the **bigplanetsupport** site from the list.

2.	To add a bookmark to this page, click the **Favorites** button, 🌟, and then click the **Add to favorites** button, `Add to favorites ▾`.

📥 *Alternatively, click* **Favorites** *from the* **Menu bar** *and select* **Add to favorites**.

3.	In the **Add a Favorite** dialog box, edit the text in the **Name** field to just **bigplanetsupport**.

4.	Click **Add** to add the site to your list of favourites.

5.	Click the **Hyperlinks** link then select **BBC** from the list of links.

6.	When the **BBC** home page appears, click, 🌟, then click **Add to Favorites**. Change the name to **BBC**. To add it to your list of favourites, click **Add**.

continued over

Driving Lesson 15 - Continued

7.   Close the **BBC** site tab.

8.   Enter **www.nasa.gov** in the **Address Bar**. Press <**Enter**>.

9.   Browse the **NASA** site, and then return to its home page using the button.

10.   When the **NASA** home page appears, add it to the **Favorites**. Change the name to **NASA**. To add it to your list of favourites, click **Add**.

11.   Enter **www.direct.gov.uk** in the **Address Bar**. Press <**Enter**>.

12.   This is a site which gives access to many public services from taxing your car to information on taxes and benefits. Browse the **Directgov** home page and then add it to your **Favorites** with a name of **Government**.

13.   Return to your default **Home Page** by clicking .

14.   Several sites have now been added to your bookmarks. Click to display the **Favorites Center** panel, and ensure the **Favorites** tab is selected at the top of the panel to display the list of bookmarked sites.

15.   To display any bookmarked site, simply click the entry. Click **BBC** from the entries listed to go directly to that site. By default, the new site will replace the existing current site.

16.   Click to display the **Favorites Center** panel, and then click **bigplanetsupport** from the list to go directly to that site.

17.   Return to your default **Home Page** using the button.

Driving Lesson 16 - Organising Bookmarks

▣ Park and Read

Once a **Favorites** list has been created, *Internet Explorer* allows the user to manage these links in a similar way to the way *Windows* manages files. Favourites can be organised into folders, and moved, renamed or deleted.

℞ Manoeuvres

1. Click ⭐ to display the **Favorites Center** panel, then click 📌 to pin it to the left of the window.

2. Click the drop down arrow at the right of the **Add to Favorites** button and select **Organize favorites**. The **Organize Favorites** dialog box is displayed.

> ℹ **Organize Favorites** *is also an option from the* **Favorites** *menu.*

3. Click the **New Folder** button.

4. A new folder is created. Type the name **Information** and press <**Enter**>.

5. Select the **BBC** page and click on the **Move** button.

6. Select the newly created folder, **Information**, then click **OK**. The **BBC** link is moved to the new folder.

7. Select the **NASA** page from the **Favorites** list and click **Rename**.

8. Change the name of the entry to **Space Exploration**, then press <**Enter**>.

> ℹ *To delete a link or a folder (and all of its contents), just select it and click the* **Delete** *button. There will be a confirmation prompt if deleting a folder.*

9. Click **Close** in the dialog box to remove it.

10. There will now be an **Information** folder in the **Favorites Center**. Click on it to display the contents (the **BBC** site link).

11. Close the **Favorites Center** but leave the browser window open.

Driving Lesson 17 - The Favorites Bar

🄿 Park and Read

The addresses of favourite sites can also be added to the **Favorites bar**. This bar can be permanently displayed above the main view so that selected sites can be accessed instantly without even displaying the **Favorites Center**.

🄿 Manoeuvres

1. If the **Favorites bar** is not displayed, right click in a blank space at the top of the window and make sure **Favorites bar** is selected.

2. The link to the **Directgov** site is to be added to the **Favorites bar**. Right click on the **Government** link from the **Favorites Center** and select **Add to Favorites bar** from the shortcut menu.

3. The bookmark is copied to the **Favorites bar**. Notice that it still appears in the **Favorites Center**.

ℹ️ *Links can be _moved_ to the **Favorites bar** using the **Move** command in the **Organize Favorites** dialog box (the **Favorites bar** is just another folder).*

ℹ️ *To add any site immediately to the bar as you're viewing it, click **Add to Favorites Bar**, ⭐.*

4. The currently viewed site can be easily added to the **Favorites bar**. Make sure the **BBC** site is displayed. Either click the **Add to Favorites bar** button, ⭐, or drag the small icon to the left of the **BBC** web address down to a blank part of the **Favorites bar** and release.

Drag this

Add to Favorites Bar

5. It is easy to remove entries from the **Favorites bar**. For example, right click on the **BBC** entry on the **Favorites bar** and select **Delete** from the shortcut menu. The link will be removed (from the **Favorites bar** only).

6. Leave the *IE9* window open for the next Driving Lesson.

Driving Lesson 18 - Browsing History

▣ Park and Read

As you are browsing, a record is kept of all the web pages visited. This is known as a **browsing history**. The **Address Bar** can be used to return to previously visited pages. **History** also allows quick and easy access to previously visited web sites. By default *Explorer* keeps a record of the sites visited within the past 20 days, although this period can be altered to suit the user's personal requirements. It is also possible to display the history records in different ways and to clear this history at <u>any</u> time.

⌒ Manoeuvres

1. Click the drop down arrow at the right of the **Address Bar**, ⊡.

This is a sample display. Yours will look different.

2. There is a list of recently typed addresses, a list of recently visited pages (**History**) and a list of visited **Favorites** pages. The **History** and **Favorites** lists can be expanded by clicking the ⊡ buttons. Click on any entry to go directly to that page.

3. Open the **Favorites Center** and select the **History** tab. Make sure **View By Date** is selected. All sites visited (up to the default history time limit) are grouped into time periods.

4. Click on any of the time periods to see the sites visited during this time.

5. Click on any site listed to see the individual pages visited.

continued over

Driving Lesson 18 - Continued

6.   Click on any page listed to display that page.

7.   Click the drop down arrow at the top of the **History** panel to see the options for displaying history entries. Try a few options and then return to **View By Date**.

8.   Any individual entry in the history can be deleted. Right click on an entry in the list and select **Delete** (select **Yes** to confirm the action if prompted).

9.   Click the **Tools** button, , and select **Internet options**. Make sure the **General** tab is selected in the dialog box.

i   *Delete browsing history is also an option from the **Tools** menu.*

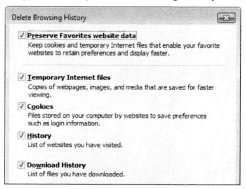

10.   Select **Delete** from the **Browsing history** section. A dialog box with options for deleting various aspects of browsing history is displayed.

11.   Make sure the top 5 boxes are checked and click **Delete**. After a short delay a message will be displayed to show that the history has been deleted. Close the dialog box and the message.

12.   Look at **History** in the **Favorites Center** – there should be no entries.

13.   Check the **Address Bar** drop down list. This has also been cleared of all history. Only **Favorites** are left.

Driving Lesson 19 - Stop and Refresh Downloads

▣ Park and Read

When a web page is opened, it automatically begins to **download**. This can often take a long time (for example, if there are a lot of graphics). The download can be stopped if necessary, and the **Refresh** feature will start the download again. Some web sites are being constantly changed or updated, even as they are viewed. Using **Refresh** will also ensure that the most up to date version of the site is being viewed.

Manoeuvres

1. Enter the web address **www.nationalgeographic.com** in the **Address Bar** and press <**Enter**>.

2. As the graphics are being downloaded, click the **Stop** button on the **Address Bar**. The download will halt.

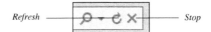

Refresh ———— *Stop*

3. Click the **Refresh** button. The downloading begins again. If any information on the page has changed, the latest version will be displayed.

4. Use the **Favorites Centre** to display the **BBC** site.

5. Use [←] to return to the **National Geographic** site. The download may be faster, because the images downloaded previously may still be available on your computer as **Temporary Internet Files**.

6. **Refresh** can be useful when viewing pages where content may be changing quickly, for example, webcams (live images from cameras which are displayed on a web page). Visit the site **www.bbc.co.uk/england/webcams/** which features webcam displays from around the country.

7. Select an option location, e.g. **Traffic**, and click on a webcam display where there may be some visible activity.

8. A new image is transmitted every few minutes. Click **Refresh**, [↻], every minute or so to see the most recent image when it becomes available.

ℹ️ *There are webcams on many other sites, e.g. **earthcam.com**. Note that some webcams are live video streams and therefore do not need refreshing.*

9. Click [🏠] to return to your default **Home Page**.

Driving Lesson 20 - Revision

This covers the features introduced in this section. Try not to refer to the preceding Driving Lessons while completing it.

1. Type the address **www.sainsburys.co.uk** in the **Address Bar**.

2. Use hyperlinks to view topics of interest to you.

3. Use the **Back** button, , to return to the **Sainsbury's** home page.

4. Bookmark the page. Name it **Sainsbury's**.

5. Now visit the **CNN** home page (**www.cnn.com**).

6. Bookmark the home page.

7. Create a folder called **News** and move the **CNN** link into it.

8. Navigate the **CNN** site using hyperlinks, and .

9. The **CNN** home page is updated hourly. **Refresh** the page to see if it has changed.

10. Add the **CNN** home page link to your **Favorites bar**. Make sure it is still shown in the **Favorites Center** list (in **News**).

11. Display your **History** in the **Favorites Center**.

12. Display the **History** in alphabetical order of site.

13. Remove the **Sainsbury's** entries from the **Favorites** list.

14. Delete the folder **News** and all its contents.

15. Remove **CNN** from the **Favorites bar**.

16. Return to your default **Home Page**.

If you experienced any difficulty completing the Revision, refer back to the Driving Lessons in this section. Then redo the Revision.

Driving Lesson 21 - Revision

This covers the features introduced in this section. Try not to refer to the preceding Driving Lessons while completing it.

1. Go to **www.bbc.co.uk**.

2. Use some of the hyperlinks to browse the site.

3. Go to your default **Home Page**.

4. Use the **Address Bar** list to visit the **BBC** page (or enter its web address manually if it does not appear).

5. View the site **www.bigplanetsupport.co.uk**.

6. View the **Hyperlinks** page and follow the link to **Google Search**.

7. Add links to the **Google** site to both the **Favorites Center** and the **Favorites bar**.

8. Remove the links if you wish.

9. Display a list of sites visited today.

10. Clear the browsing history.

11. Return to your default **Home Page**.

If you experienced any difficulty completing the Revision, refer back to the Driving Lessons in this section. Then redo the Revision.

Once you are confident with the features, complete the Record of Achievement Matrix referring to the section at the end of the guide. Only when competent move on to the next Section.

Section 3
Browsing the Web

By the end of this Section you should be able to:

Browse the Web using Search Engines

Define Searches using Search Criteria

Use Subject Directories

Use Site Searches

Find Text on a Page

Use Internet Options

Complete a Web Form

To gain an understanding of the above features, work through the **Driving Lessons** in this **Section**.

For each **Driving Lesson**, read the **Park and Read** instructions, without touching the keyboard, then work through the numbered steps of the **Manoeuvres** on the computer. Complete the **Revision Exercise(s)** at the end of the section to test your knowledge.

Driving Lesson 22 - Search Engines

▣ Park and Read

A **search engine** is a facility connected to a vast database. Once the user has entered key words, the search engine will select every site on its database containing those words. Some current search engines are:

Google	**www.google.com**
Bing	**www.bing.com**
Yahoo	**www.yahoo.co.uk**

There are many others available, however, and new ones appear all the time. *Google* is the most popular at the time of writing. As these products are being constantly developed, their current appearance may differ from the screen shots shown here. Each search engine will feature a **search box**, however, where the user enters details of the subject they want to find.

⟳ Manoeuvres

1. As an example of a search engine, enter **www.google.co.uk** in the **Address Bar** and press **<Enter>**. The **Google** search engine is launched.

2. In the **search box**, enter **shark**. The window changes as you type. Ignore any predictive suggestions that may appear as you are typing.

3. Click on the **Search** button or press **<Enter>**.

 *In other search engines this may be a **Web Search** button or an icon,* .

4. **Google** will show links to every site on its database which contains this word. The number of results is also usually displayed.

5. Some commercially sponsored sites and relevant advertisements may be listed first or in a panel on the right. Select the first 'real' web site match by clicking on it, and browse the site.

6. Click the **Back** button until the first page of results is displayed again.

continued over

Driving Lesson 22 - Continued

7.   Different types of result can be specified. Find an **Images** link above the search box or on the left of the window and click on it. Now only image results are listed.

8.   Click on the **News** link in the same area. Now only news items about sharks are listed.

9.   Click the **Back** button until the **Google** home page is displayed again (with no results shown).

10. The predictive feature of search engines can be quite useful. Suppose you are looking for hotels in Windermere in the Lake District. Slowly type **windermere** into the search box. As each letter is typed, some relevant predictions are listed below the box.

11. Before long, **windermere hotels** will appear in the list. Click on the entry as soon as it appears to display results for hotels in Windermere.

12. Very specific searches can be made. If you want to know if wasp stings are acidic or alkaline, highlight the current text in the search box and start to type the question: **are wasp stings acidic**.

13. After a few key strokes, the relevant question will appear in the prediction list (along with some other fascinating questions). Click on it to see a list of informative sites.

14. Return to your default **Home Page** by clicking the **Home** button, .

15. Enter **www.yahoo.com** in the **Address Bar** and press <**Enter**>.

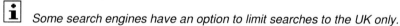

Some search engines have an option to limit searches to the UK only.

16. Try the **shark** and the **windermere** searches with this search engine. The results will be similar.

17. Return to your default **Home Page** by clicking the **Home** button, then enter **www.bing.com** in the **Address Bar** and press <**Enter**>.

18. Try the shark and the windermere searches with this search engine then return to your home page.

Driving Lesson 23 - Search Criteria

▣ Park and Read

The previous Driving Lesson demonstrates a common problem encountered by Internet users: a search can produce hundreds of thousands of **"hits"**, not all of them relevant to the intended subject. It is possible to narrow the search considerably by using certain criteria.

Specify the location	Select **UK only** as a pre-search option.
Include more key words	Enter more than one key word, e.g. **oscar director 1976**.
Exclude words	Enter a - before an unwanted word, e.g. **french wine -champagne**.
Use phrases	To search for an exact phrase rather than just the constituent word, use speech marks, e.g. **"Tom and Jerry"** or **"The Battle of Hastings"**.

 Manoeuvres

1. Open the search engine of your choice. Imagine you need information on Captain Cook the explorer. Type **cook** in the search box and press <**Enter**>. There will be a large number of results found and most of them will not be connected with the explorer. Make a note of the number of results found.

2. Change the entry in the search box to **captain cook** and press <**Enter**>. There will be fewer results (make a note of the number) and they now seem more relevant.

3. Change the entry in the search box to **"captain cook"** and press <**Enter**>. Now only pages where the two words appear as a phrase will be found so there will be fewer results.

ⓘ *This does not make much practical difference in this particular search, as the previous search lists the most relevant results first anyway, i.e. those where the two words appear together.*

4. If you are particularly interested in his ship, change the entry in the search box to **"captain cook" resolution** and press <**Enter**>. Now only pages that specifically mention his ship, HMS Resolution will be listed.

5. Having heard some IT technicians talking about nelly moser you decide to find out what it means. Type **nelly moser** in your search engine search box and press <**Enter**>. It's a garden shrub, a type of clematis.

continued over

Driving Lesson 23 - Continued

6. To see if it has any other meaning without having to browse through all the results, change the entry in the search box to **nelly moser -clematis** and press <**Enter**>. All results which include the word **clematis** are now omitted. These results seem more appropriate.

7. Type your name in the search box, and press <**Enter**>. All pages with your individual names (e.g. **Ted** or **Smith**) anywhere on the page will be located, but those with the names together (**Ted Smith**) will be shown first.

8. Now enter your name in quotes. The number of matches should have reduced.

i   *Some search engines also have an **Advanced Search** option which can be used to find web pages published in a specific language or within a certain date range.*

9. Try a few more searches for topics that interest you. Try to locate and use the advanced search features of the search engine.

10. When you are finished, click the **Home** button to return to your default **Home Page**.

Driving Lesson 24 - Subject Directories

P Park and Read

There will be many occasions when a user wants to retrieve information from the web, but does not have a specific address. It is still possible to find relevant information by using a **subject directory**.

An alternative to a search engine, a **subject directory** classifies web sites by subject. Clicking on the relevant subject will take the user into progressively more detailed lists, from which a selection can be made. Advantages of using subject directories are that they generally contain good quality sites, consequently they contain fewer sites than search engines and therefore save time. Most of the search engines also contain these directories.

Manoeuvres

1. Search for the **open directory project** in your search engine (or enter the web address **www.dmoz.org**). At the time of writing, this is a popular subject directory. A page similar to that shown below appears.

 If this website does not work, try searching for another subject directory.

The web organized by topic into categories.		
Arts Music, Movies, Performing Arts, ...	**Home** Cooking, Family, Gardening, ...	**Regional** North America, Europe, Oceania, ...
Business Industrial Goods and Services, Finance, ...	**Kids and Teens** International, School Time, Games, ...	**Science** Biology, Social Sciences, Technology, ...
Computers Software, Internet, Programming, ...	**News** Newspapers, Media, Colleges and Universities, ...	**Shopping** Home and Garden, Crafts, Sports, ...
Games Video Games, Roleplaying, Board Games, ...	**Recreation** Pets, Outdoors, Food, ...	**Society** Religion and Spirituality, Law, Issues, ...
Health Conditions and Diseases, Medicine, Animal, ...	**Reference** Education, Biography, Museums, ...	**Sports** Soccer, Equestrian, Football, ...
World Deutsch, Español, Français, Italiano, Japanese, Korean, Nederlands, Polski, Svenska, ...		

2. Under the **Arts** heading, click on the hyperlink **Movies**. Then select the **Actors and Actresses** category. An A-Z list will be displayed at the top of the page.

 It is possible some of these links may have changed. If so, replace them with links of your choice.

3. Click on the letter **F**, then select the hyperlink **Fiennes, Ralph**.

4. Select any page from the list. Browse the page.

5. Click [🏠] to return to your default **Home Page**.

Driving Lesson 25 - Site Searches

▣ Park and Read

Apart from search engines, which search the whole web, many individual sites have there own search feature which will reference any information within that site. For sites containing a lot of information, such as the BBC or CNN, this can be a useful feature.

There are many online reference books, encyclopaedias and dictionaries available such as **wikipedia.org** and **webdictionary.co.uk**, which are free, and **Britannica.com**, which requires a subscription for full access. In sites such as these, the internal search feature is very powerful.

⌕ Manoeuvres

1. Display the **bigplanetsupport** home page in your *Internet Explorer* window.

2. There is a search box near the top right of the page. Type in the word **outlook**.

3. Click **Search this site**. All instances of the word, throughout the whole site, will be listed. Click on the required page link ⬚ E-mail, to display the whole page containing the selected word.

4. Read the information on the page, and then return to your default **Home Page**.

5. Enter **www.en.wikipedia.org** in the **Address Bar** and press <**Enter**>. This is written by volunteers worldwide - beware - 100% accuracy cannot be guaranteed because of this, although topics are generally of a good quality.

6. In the **search** box, enter **blackbird**. Ignore any listed suggestions and press <**Enter**>. A large list of possible topics is listed.

7. Browse the list to see the various topics available, then click the top one, for the **Common Blackbird**. A comprehensive page of information is displayed.

8. Use the **Home** button to return to your default **Home Page**.

Driving Lesson 26 - Finding Text

⊞ Park and Read

Internet Explorer has a **Find** facility which will search the current page for specific text. Note that this is an *Internet Explorer* feature, and therefore available for <u>any</u> selected web page.

↱ Manoeuvres

1. Display the **bigplanetsupport** home page. Make sure the **Menu bar** is displayed (see Driving lesson 8).

2. Click the **E-mail** link on the left of the page (you may have to expand the **Information** link first).

3. Click **Edit** from the **Menu bar** and select **Find on this page**.

4. The **Find** bar appears. This bar will remain in view until it is closed or the *IE9* session is closed.

5. In the **Find** box, enter **message**. All matches on the page are highlighted. The first match should be in view and have a different colour highlight.

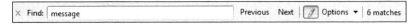

6. Click **Next**. *Explorer* will highlight the next occurrence of the word **message** on the page and ensure that it is in view.

7. Click **Next** again. Repeat this action until the first occurrence of the word is highlighted again, indicating that the search has been completed.

8. Close the **Find** bar by clicking the **Close the Find bar** button, ⊠, at the left end of the bar.

9. Go to your default **Home Page**.

Driving Lesson 27 - Internet Options

▣ Park and Read

Explorer's **Internet Options** allow the user to change some of its elements to their individual preference, the default home page, for example, and the number of days pages are kept in the history, can both be changed. All recently viewed pages and objects are kept in a cache on the computer's hard drive, so that if they need to be viewed again, they can be accessed quickly without necessarily downloading them again. These **Temporary Internet files** can take up a lot of space on the hard drive, but can be deleted (if desired) from within **Internet Options**.

Internet connection settings and the current program settings used by *Explorer* for e-mail and personal information can also be changed.

↱ Manoeuvres

1. Click the **Tools** button, [⚙], on the *Internet Explorer* window and select **Internet options**. Make sure the **General** tab is selected in the dialog box.

ℹ️ *Internet options can also be selected from **Tools** on the **Menu bar** and the **Command bar**.*

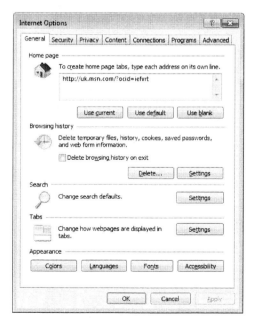

continued over

Driving Lesson 27 - Continued

2. In the **Home page** section, change the default address to **http://www.google.com**, then click **OK**.

3. Click [icon]. Note how your default **Home Page** is now **Google**.

4. Click **Tools** then **Internet options**. Select **Delete** from the **Browsing history** section to display the **Delete Browsing History** dialog box as seen previously.

5. Check only the **Temporary Internet Files** box and click **Delete**. This action removes all temporary files but this may slow down subsequent site downloads (because all data will need to be retrieved again).

[i] *A message will appear when the deletion is complete.*

6. Select **Settings** from the **Browsing history** section. Read all the options which are displayed then set the **Days to keep pages in history** to an appropriate number for your personal needs (for example, 14 days). Click **OK**.

7. Select **Settings** from the **Tabs** section. Read all the options which are available then click **Cancel** to return.

8. Look at the buttons in the **Appearance** section.

9. Click each button in turn, read the options available then click **Cancel** to return.

10. Select the **Content** tab at the top of the dialog box. This tab is where **Parental Controls** and **Content Advisor** settings can be defined. Do not change any of these settings without expert advice.

11. Select the **Connections** tab and view the various connection options that are available. Do not change any of these settings without expert advice.

12. Go back to the **General** tab and click **OK**.

13. Close the **deleting** confirmation message.

Driving Lesson 28 - Security

▣ Park and Read

Internet Options allows you to apply settings which control the security of your web browsing. This covers control over which downloads are allowed in various situations, which **Cookies** (see Driving Lesson 3) will be accepted, and which **Pop-ups** will be allowed. Pop-ups are windows that pop up in the middle of your screen, usually containing advertisements. Some are helpful, but others can be annoying or can lead to downloading spyware or adware.

There are also options to rate and control the type of content that can be viewed, including **Parental Control** settings.

⌕ Manoeuvres

1. Click the **Tools** button, ⬚, and select **Internet options**. Select the **Security** tab in the dialog box.

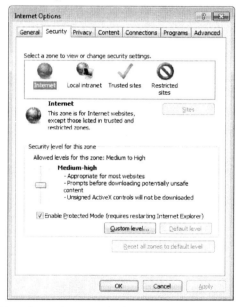

2. The vertical slider allows the security level to be set separately for each of the four zones in the upper panel. The picture above shows that a **Medium-high** security level is set for **Internet** websites. Click the other zones to see the default security settings.

3. To see the settings for cookies, select the **Privacy** tab from the **Internet Options** dialog box.

continued over

Driving Lesson 28 - Continued

4. The **Settings** slider has 5 settings: **Block All Cookies**, **High**, **Medium High**, **Medium** (default), **Low** and **Accept All Cookies**. Change the slider position to see details of other levels of blocking, but return it to its original position unless you are confident of the implications of changing it.

5. The **Pop-up Blocker** option should be on by default. If you want to allow pop-ups from a particular web site, click the **Settings** button, type the address into the box provided and click **Add**. To block pop-ups, select **High** from the **Blocking level** drop down list.

 *Pop-ups can be allowed by clicking the **Information Bar** on the page where they are blocked.*

6. Click **Close** to remove the dialog box.

7. Select the **Content** tab from the **Internet Options** dialog box. **Parental Controls** and **Content Advisor** can be controlled from here. Do not change anything here unless you are confident of the implications.

8. Click **Cancel** to close the dialog box without saving changes in this instance.

9. Click **Home,** and leave your default **Home Page** open.

Driving Lesson 29 - Completing a Web Form

▣ Park and Read

From time to time when you are using the Internet, especially if you are buying goods, it will be necessary to complete online forms. These forms nearly always consist of text boxes that require information to be typed in and drop down lists from which selections can be made. There may also be a **Submit** button and a **Reset** or **Clear** button. The **Submit** button sends the form to its destination and the **Reset** button clears the form without sending it.

Manoeuvres

1. Display the **www.bigplanetsupport.co.uk** home page.

2. Click **Online Forms** in the **Navigation** pane on the left. The page that appears contains links to various online forms for you to try.

 The online forms provided are for demonstration purposes only and are typical of the many web-based forms used by websites on the Web. Even though the details you enter here are not sent to anybody or recorded anywhere, you should not enter any real personal details.

3. Select **Feedback Form** from the main panel. A sample form is displayed in a new browser tab.

4. This form includes a variety of methods for entering data; text boxes, drop down menus, check boxes and option selections. Complete the **Name** and **E-mail Address** text boxes.

5. Right click on the form and select **Refresh**. All data is cleared from the form, ready to start again. This is used when mistakes have been made and it is easier to start again.

6. Re-enter the details, then complete the rest of the form. Entries with an * after them are essential and the form cannot be submitted without completing these fields.

7. When complete click the **Submit** button.

8. Instead of transmitting the data this simulation displays a confirmation page. Click **Go Back to the form** then close the **Form** tab.

9. Look at the other sample forms to see the sort of fields you may encounter.

10. Close any open **Form** tabs and return to your default **Home Page**.

Driving Lesson 30 - Revision

This covers the features introduced in this section. Try not to refer to the preceding Driving Lessons while completing it.

1. Change your default home page to **www.bbc.co.uk**.

2. Search for information on cheap flights to **Europe** using **Google**.

3. Search for information about **ECDL**. Use the search criteria **"ECDL"**.

4. Were more or less than one million matches found?

5. Go to **Google's** home page.

6. Enter the correct criteria to search for information about **hungarian recipes** (search for the complete phrase) but not **goulash**.

7. Were any matches found?

8. Enter a search for the phrase **russian hamsters**.

9. View one of the matched pages and use the **Find** feature to see if you can find some information about their diet.

10. Close the **Find bar**.

11. Return to **Google** and search for web pages about your favourite film star or musician.

12. Change your default home page to a site of your own choosing.

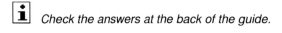 *Check the answers at the back of the guide.*

If you experienced any difficulty completing the Revision, refer back to the Driving Lessons in this section. Then redo the Revision.

Driving Lesson 31 - Revision

This covers the features introduced in this section. Try not to refer to the preceding Driving Lessons while completing it.

1. Go to any search engine home page.

2. Use search criteria to find **images** of the **Sahara Desert**.

3. Use any search engine to find out how to create a family tree.

4. Find out how to make a **tequila sunrise**.

5. See if you can find a web site dedicated to **Vietnamese pot bellied pigs**.

6. Bookmark the page.

7. Look for a web site specialising in holidays to **Iceland**.

8. Find out the cost of a return flight from **Heathrow** to **Paris**.

9. Go to your default **Home Page**.

If you experienced any difficulty completing the Revision, refer back to the Driving Lessons in this section. Then redo the Revision.

Once you are confident with the features, complete the Record of Achievement Matrix referring to the section at the end of the guide. Only when competent move on to the next Section.

Section 4
Saving and Printing

By the end of this Section you should be able to:

Save a Web Page

Duplicate Web Page Items

Modify Page Setup

Preview and Print a Page

Print a Search Result

Download Files

To gain an understanding of the above features, work through the **Driving Lessons** in this **Section**.

For each **Driving Lesson**, read the **Park and Read** instructions, without touching the keyboard, then work through the numbered steps of the **Manoeuvres** on the computer. Complete the **Revision Exercise(s)** at the end of the section to test your knowledge.

Driving Lesson 32 - Saving a Web Page

🄿 Park and Read

Web pages can be saved directly from the Internet in the same way as other files or folders and stored locally on your computer.

🖑 Manoeuvres

1.   Display the **www.bigplanetsupport.co.uk** home page.

2.   Click on the **Image Gallery** hyperlink on the left. To save this page, click the **Tools** button, [⚙], select **File**, then **Save as**. The **Save Webpage** dialog box is displayed.

ℹ️   *Save as can also be selected by clicking the **File** menu or the **Page** command button if these are available.*

3.   Select **Documents** from the left panel as the save location. Change the **File name** to **Hyperlinks** by overtyping the existing name, and make sure **Save as type** shows **Webpage, complete**.

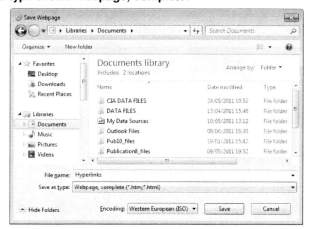

4.   Click **Save**.

5.   To save the page as a text file, repeat the **Save as** process, but enter **Webtext** as the **File name** and select **Text file (*.txt)** for **Save as type**.

6.   Click **Save**, then click **Home** to return to your default **Home Page**.

7.   Open **Documents** from the **Start** menu. The files **Webtext.txt** and **Hyperlinks.htm** file will be listed. Double click the **Hyperlinks** file name and it will be displayed in *Explorer* with a new tab.

8.   Close the new tab and close the **Documents** window.

Driving Lesson 33 - Copying Web Page Items

🅿 Park and Read

It is possible to copy text and images from a web page and then to paste them into a document. Be aware of copyright restrictions before using any objects taken from the Internet.

Manoeuvres

1. Display the **www.bigplanetsupport.co.uk** home page.

2. Make sure the **Image Gallery** link at the left of the page is expanded and click **Places**. To copy any image, right click on it and select **Copy** from the shortcut menu.

3. Start *Word* (for example, **Start | All Programs | Microsoft Office | Microsoft Word 2010**).

4. Click **Paste**, [Paste], or press <**Ctrl V**> to place the duplicated image in the document.

5. Press <**Enter**> to start a new line and use the **Taskbar** to return to the **bigplanetsupport** site.

6. Right click in the **Address Bar** to highlight the full address.

7. Select **Copy** from the shortcut menu.

8. Switch back to *Word*. Type in **Why not try visiting** and then click **Paste** to complete the sentence.

9. The web page address of the **CiA** web page is pasted into the document. Press <**Enter**> at the end of the copied address. Notice how the address becomes blue and underlined, indicating that it is now a hyperlink.

10. Hold down the <**Ctrl**> key and click the hyperlink to open the web page. The page opens in another tab in *IE9*.

11. Close this new *Internet Explorer* tab.

12. Click the **Image Gallery** link. Click and drag to select the first paragraph of text on the page. Right click on the selected text and select **Copy**,

13. Switch back to *Word*, and with the cursor under the address pasted earlier, press <**Enter**> and paste the copied text onto the page.

14. Save the document in **Documents** as **Copied** and close *Word*.

Driving Lesson 34 - Page Setup

🅿 Park and Read

If necessary, the **Page Setup** (margins, etc.) of a web page can be changed before printing. You may occasionally want to change the size of paper used, e.g. to **A5**. This will mean the settings must also be adjusted to print the information in the correct position on the paper.

Manoeuvres

1. Make sure the **bigplanetsupport** site is displayed and click the **Home** link.

2. Click the **Tools** button, 🔧, select **Print**, then **Page setup**. The **Page Setup** dialog box is displayed.

ℹ *Page setup can also be selected from the **File** menu or the **Print** command button if these are available.*

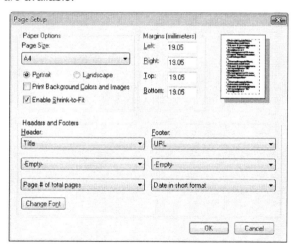

3. Look at the available settings. Change the **Orientation** of the printed page by selecting the **Landscape** option.

4. Change all margins: **Left**, **Right**, **Top** and **Bottom** to **25mm** by deleting the number in the boxes and entering the new measurement.

5. Click the drop down arrow at the right of the **Page Size** box to see the range of page size options available. These options depend on the default printer. Make sure the option is set as **A4**.

6. Click **OK** to apply the new settings and move on to the next Driving Lesson.

Driving Lesson 35 - Printing a Web Page

▣ Park and Read

With *Internet Explorer* you can print pages, or parts of pages, directly from the Internet. The user can decide exactly which parts of the web page to print. If the page is **framed**, individual frames or selected frames can be printed, or the page can be printed as it appears on the screen. It is also possible to print all linked documents, or a table of links. A page can be previewed before printing.

⤺ Manoeuvres

1. With the **bigplanetsupport** site open, display the **Home** page.

2. Click the **Tools** button, 🔩, select **Print**, then **Print preview**. A preview of how the page will print is displayed. Click 🔳 to close the preview.

ℹ️ *Print and Print preview can also be selected from the **File** menu or the drop down arrow on the **Print** command button 🖨 ▾ if these are available. Clicking the **Print** button itself will print the current page on the default printer with no further intervention.*

3. Click the **Tools** button, 🔩, select **Print**, then **Print** again to display the print dialog box. Select the appropriate printer, set the **Print Range** to **All**, and make sure that the **Number of copies** is set to **1**.

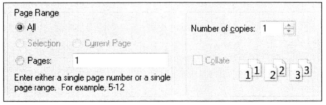

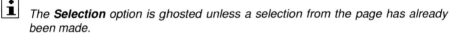

ℹ️ *The **Selection** option is ghosted unless a selection from the page has already been made.*

4. Click the **Print** button in the dialog box to print the page.

5. Click and drag to select the **Home** heading and the paragraphs of text below it.

6. Click 🔩 again, then **Print** and **Print** again. Select **Selection** from the **Print Range** and click **Print**. Only the selected text will be printed.

7. Display the **Google** home page and then the **Tools** button. Select **Print** then **Print** again. Click the **Options** tab and select **Print table of links**.

8. Click **Print**. The page is printed plus a page detailing all of the links found on the web page.

Driving Lesson 36 - Printing a Search Result

▣ Park and Read

If a list of search results has been retrieved and the user does not wish to spend online time searching through them, the results can be printed. This means that any appropriate sites can be marked and then browsed later.

⌢ Manoeuvres

1. Use any search engine and enter the following search: **"Garden gnomes"**. An example is shown below.

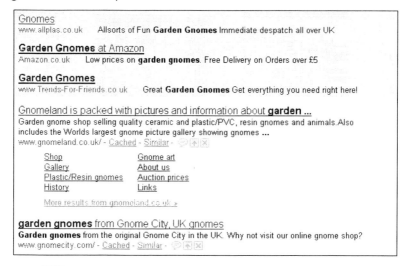

2. Click ⚙, then **Print** and then **Page Setup**. Change the **Orientation** back to **Portrait** and make sure the page size is **A4**.

3. Press <**Ctrl P**> (this is an alternative method of displaying the **Print** dialog box). Make sure **Page Range** is set to **All**.

ℹ️ *In the **Print** dialog box, the **Page Range** setting refers to printed pages, not web pages. The **Print** command only ever prints the <u>current</u> web page, although this may require many printed pages.*

4. Click **Print** to print the displayed page. It may be spread over two sheets.

5. To print the next page of results, move to next page in the *IE9* window and then run **Print** again.

6. Return to your default **Home Page**.

Driving Lesson 37 - Downloading Files

🅿 Park and Read

Many types of files, including sound and video files, can be downloaded from the Internet and viewed or played. Downloaded files can also be permanently saved to either the hard drive of your computer or to another external device. Be aware of copyright restrictions before using any objects taken from the Internet (it is safe to assume that all items obtained from the Internet are subject to copyright restrictions unless otherwise stated).

🅁 Manoeuvres

1.   Display the **www.bigplanetsupport.co.uk** home page and click on the **Downloads** hyperlink at the left of the page.

2.   Click on the hyperlink **Berlioz.wav**. A message will ask whether you want to **open** or **save** the object. Click **Open**.

3.   After a delay while the file is security checked, your media player application (*Windows Media Player* by default) will open and the file will start to play.

Pause/Play

Volume Control

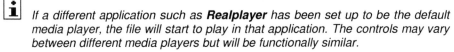

> ℹ️ *If a different application such as **Realplayer** has been set up to be the default media player, the file will start to play in that application. The controls may vary between different media players but will be functionally similar.*

4.   The file is stored in the **Temporary Internet Files** cache. When the clip has finished playing, the **Pause** button becomes the **Play** button. Press this (or click the **Play again** option) to hear the music again. It is now playing from the cache in your computer, not the web site.

continued over

Driving Lesson 37 - Continued

 *The **Berlioz** file has not been permanently downloaded. It is stored in the **Temporary Internet Files** cache. It is not readily accessible and when this is deleted, the file will be lost. The following actions will show how to save objects permanently.*

5. Close the **Media Player** and click on the hyperlink **Berlioz.wav** again. This time select **Save** from the message. The music file is saved into your **Downloads** folder without any further intervention.

6. To have control over the location of the saved file, right click on the **Berlioz.wav** link and select **Save target as** from the shortcut menu.

7. In the **Save As** dialog box make sure the save location is set to **Documents**, leave the **Name** and **Type** as they are and click **Save**.

8. Click the **Start** button and click on **Documents**. A copy of the **berlioz.wav** file has been downloaded into this folder and will remain there until deleted, even after the Internet connection is closed.

9. Any object can be downloaded in this manner. Right click the **Testimonial.doc** link on the **Downloads** page and select **Save target as** from the shortcut menu.

10. In the **Save As** dialog box make sure the save location is set to **Documents**, leave the **Name** and **Type** as they are and click **Save**.

11. Right click the **Ocean.avi** link on the **Downloads** page and select **Save target as** from the shortcut menu.

12. In the **Save As** dialog box make sure the save location is set to **Documents**, leave the **Name** and **Type** as they are and click **Save**.

13. Click on the **Places** hyperlink at the left of the **bigplanetsupport** page. Right click on any image and select **Save picture as**.

14. Change the download location from **Pictures** to **Documents** and change the **File** name to **sample**. Click **Save**.

15. Click the **Start** button and open **Documents**. The files **berlioz.wav**, **ocean.avi**, **sample.jpg** and **Testimonial.doc** will be listed.

16. Double click the **ocean.avi** entry to start the demonstration movie. Close the media player when it is finished.

17. Delete the files **berlioz.wav**, **ocean.avi**, **sample.jpg** and **Testimonial.doc** from **Documents**.

18. Use the **Navigation** panel on the left to change the location to the **Downloads** folder and delete the **berlioz.wav** file that was saved there.

19. Close the window showing the **Downloads** contents.

Driving Lesson 38 - Revision

This covers the features introduced in this section. Try not to refer to the preceding Driving Lessons while completing it.

1. Go to the **NASA** home page (**www.nasa.gov**).

2. Use hyperlinks to find a page that interests you.

3. Save the web page as a file.

4. Use a search engine to search for web pages about homeopathy.

5. Print the first two <u>web</u> pages of the search result.

6. Go to **www.ciatraining.co.uk**.

7. Change the page orientation to **Landscape**.

8. Print one copy of page **1**.

9. Go to **www.bigplanetsupport.co.uk** and click the **Downloads** link.

10. Play the **Apollo.wav** sound file.

11. Save the **Apollo.wav** sound file in **Documents**.

12. View the web page saved from the **NASA** site in step 3 (this may not look as good as it did originally as a lot of the formatting will be lost).

13. Close any open programs and disconnect from the Internet.

If you experienced any difficulty completing the Revision, refer back to the Driving Lessons in this section. Then redo the Revision.

Driving Lesson 39 - Revision

This covers the features introduced in this section. Try not to refer to the preceding Driving Lessons while completing it.

1. Go to **www.nasa.gov**.

2. Right click on any image.

3. Save the image in your pictures folder\library as **nasapic**.

4. Choose a link to another page and save the resulting web page in your documents folder\library as **nasapage**.

5. Return to your **Home Page**.

6. Open your pictures folder\library (in *Windows Explorer*) and display the image **nasapic**.

7. Close the image and delete it.

8. Open your documents folder\library and display the page **nasapage**.

9. Close the page and delete it.

10. Close any open windows.

11. Close *IE9*, disconnecting if you have a dial up connection.

If you experienced any difficulty completing the Revision, refer back to the Driving Lessons in this section. Then redo the Revision.

Once you are confident with the features, complete the Record of Achievement Matrix referring to the section at the end of the guide. Only when competent move on to the next Section.

Answers

Driving Lesson 10

Step 1   **www** stands for **world wide web**.

Step 2   The main programming language used on the Internet is **HTML**.

Step 3   Traditionally, a connection (usually a telephone line), a modem and ISP (Internet Service Provider), although Broadband connections now allow more direct access using devices other than modems.

Step 5   The **Favorites Center** includes both of these features.

Step 6   **Menu bar**, **Favorites bar** and **Command bar**.

Driving Lesson 11

Step 1   **ISP** stands for **Internet Service Provider**.

Step 2   The Internet is a worldwide network connection of computers.

Step 3   The world wide web refers to the information that exists on the Internet.

Step 4   **Cookies** are small text files that are stored on your computer when you visit a web site.

Step 5   **Encrypted** means scrambled. Can only be deciphered with a key.

Step 6   A **firewall** is a program that protects a computer from unauthorised access via the Internet.

Step 7   Secure servers are identified by a small padlock in the **Status Bar**.

Driving Lesson 30

Step 4   More than one million.

Step 6   "hungarian recipes" -goulash

Step 7   Yes, many thousand.

Glossary

Browser	The application that controls your interface with the World Wide Web.
Dial-up Connection	A method of connecting to the Internet that requires a modem on the computer dialling the number of a server.
Download	Transfers an object from a web site to the user's computer.
Favorites	A list of selected web pages that can be visited with a single mouse click.
Folder	A method of grouping together files (and other folders).
Frames	Separate areas of a single web page that each act like individual pages.
History	A list of web pages visited recently.
Home Page (1)	A site Home Page is the main page in a site, with links to all other pages.
Home Page (2)	Your default Home Page is the page displayed when the Browser starts and when you press the Home button.
Hyperlink	Text or images which can be clicked to move to a different location (usually a different web page).
Link	Abbreviation for **Hyperlink**.
Media Player	An application which plays sound or video files.
Navigation	Moving around between web sites or the pages within a site.
Offline	Without having a current connection to the Internet.
Online	Having a current connection to the Internet.
Page Range	The specific print pages to be included when printing out a large web page.
Recycle Bin	An area of storage where deleted files are held temporarily before being deleted completely.
Refresh	Redisplays the most recent version of the current page.
Search Engine	A web site that allows all other sites to be searched for specified topics.
Subfolder	A folder that is contained within another folder.

Index

Record of Achievement Matrix

This Matrix is to be used to measure your progress while working through the guide. This is a learning reinforcement process, you judge when you are competent.

Tick boxes are provided for each feature. 1 is for no knowledge, 2 some knowledge and 3 is for competent. A section is only complete when column 3 is completed for all parts of the section.

For details on sitting ECDL Examinations in your country please contact the local ECDL Licensee or visit the European Computer Driving Licence Foundation Limited web site at http://www.ecdl.org.

Tick the Relevant Boxes   **1**: No Knowledge   **2**: Some Knowledge   **3**: Competent

Section	No	Driving Lesson	1	2	3
1 Getting Started	1	Internet Theory			
	2	Internet Explorer			
	3	Security on the Internet			
	4	Connecting to the Internet			
	5	Dial-up Connection			
	6	Browser Help			
	7	Internet Explorer Screen			
	8	Views			
	9	Closing the Browser			
2 Navigation	12	Using Hyperlinks			
	13	Navigation Buttons			
	14	Using Web Addresses			
	15	Bookmarks			
	16	Organising Bookmarks			
	17	The Favorites Bar			
	18	Browsing History			
	19	Stop and Refresh Downloads			
3 Browsing the Web	22	Search Engines			
	23	Search Criteria			
	24	Subject Directories			
	25	Site Searches			
	26	Finding Text			
	27	Internet Options			
	28	Security			
	29	Completing a Web Form			
4 Saving and Printing	32	Saving a Web Page			
	33	Copying Web Page Items			
	34	Page Setup			
	35	Printing a Web Page			
	36	Printing a Search Result			
	37	Downloading Files			

Other Products from CiA Training

CiA Training is a leading publishing company which has consistently delivered the highest quality products since 1985. Our experienced in-house publishing team has developed a wide range of flexible and easy to use self-teach resources for individual learners and corporate clients all over the world.

At the time of publication, we currently offer approved ECDL materials for:

- **ECDL Syllabus 5.0**

- **ECDL Syllabus 5.0 Revision Series**

- **ECDL Advanced Syllabus 2.0**

- **ECDL Advanced Syllabus 2.0 Revision Series**

Previous syllabus versions are also available upon request.

We hope you have enjoyed using this guide and would love to hear your opinions about our materials. To let us know how we're doing, and to get up to the minute information on our current range of products, please visit us at:

www.ciatraining.co.uk

Notes